Carving Caricature Golfers

By Bill Howrilla

Fox
Chapel Publishing Co. Inc.

1970 Broad Street • East Petersburg, PA 17520 • www.foxchapelpublishing.com

Acknowledgments
Special recognition goes to Lou Vitari, a fellow member of the Chisels and
Chips Carving Club of North Pittsburgh, for paving
the way for me to work with Fox Chapel.

Publisher	Alan Giagnocavo
Book Editor	Ayleen Stellhorn
Editorial Assistant	Gretchen Bacon
Desktop Specialist	Alan Davis
Cover Design	Jon Deck

ISBN 1–56523–201-1
Library of Congress Control Number 2003116136

To order your copy of this book, please send check or money order for the cover price plus $3.50 shipping to:
Fox Books
1970 Broad Street
East Petersburg, PA 17520
1–800–457–9112

Or visit us on the web at
www.foxchapelpublishing.com

Printed in Korea
10 9 8 7 6 5 4 3 2 1

Table of CONTENTS

About the
AUTHOR

Bill Howrilla carves golfers that look as if they could walk right off their wooden bases and continue their games on the top of your desk. He has a knack for catching golfers at the height of their expressions: the thrill of sinking a difficult putt, the disbelief at missing an easy putt, the frustration of ending up in the ruff or in the sand pit…. From the best game of your life to the worst game you've ever played, any golfer will see a little bit of himself in Bill's carvings.

Bill is a native of Pittsburgh, Pennsylvania, from the North Hills area. He has been carving for almost ten years, and he has found that being a cartoonist helps a great deal to visualize the pieces he carves. His comic strip, Sergeant Stars and Stripes Forever, ran in syndication through NEA, Cleveland, Ohio, for 20 months during 1972 and 1973. It appeared in approximately 300 newspapers nationwide. His cartoons have also appeared in Leatherneck, the magazine of the Marine Corps, in the early 1990s.

His greatest carving accomplishment came in 1993 when he was asked to carve a caricature of four-star Marine Corps General Peter Pace, who is the Vice Chairman of the Joint Chiefs of Staff. Being a Marine, Bill found this an honor and a privilege. In return, he received an autographed photo and letter of recognition and thanks from the General himself.

Bill is a member of the Chisels and Chips Carving Club of North Pittsburgh.

PART ONE

ABOUT CARVING GOLFERS

Caricature (kar i ka chur) n. *The distorted representation of parts or features to produce a ridiculous effect.*

Wat I enjoy most about carving caricatures of golfers, or any other figure for that matter, is having the license and freedom to be creative. For me, it's just a matter of turning my imagination loose. I am not a golfer, but I do know enough about how the game is played from listening to my golfing friends discuss their games. I picture myself out on the course, hacking, slicing, pitching out of a sand trap, chipping onto the green, putting, missing a putt, excavating divots, landing a few balls in the lake, cussing (ooops!). Imagining how I would react in any of these situations is where I get the ideas for my golfers.

Occasionally I have entertained requests to carve personal caricatures that will be given as gifts. Whenever I do a special order of this nature, I ask for photographs of the person I am going to carve. If my client can't provide photographs, I ask specific questions about his appearance and mannerisms. What does he (or she) look like? What is his size and stature? What color is his hair? Does he wear glasses? Does he have a special outfit or hat that he frequently wears on the golf course? Is he right-handed or left-handed? I also find out what pose my client would like me to carve. Should this person be driving the ball, putting, lining up a shot or missing a putt?

I use a variety of carving knives in my caricature carving. I recommend at least one good quality detail knife with a small blade.

Palm gouges are a helpful addition to a carver's tool roll. Most of the cuts made with these tools can be duplicated with a good knife, but a specialty tool makes the process much easier.

Look for these comparison shots throughout the book. At key places in the demonstration, I will show you the in-progress carving side-by-side with the finished carving. These comparison shots will help you to visualize the end results of the cuts you are making.

Information such as this makes the gift personal, and it gives me the satisfaction of knowing that my carving will be greatly appreciated.

I then use all of this information to create an original caricature pattern. I try to capture the exaggerated expression first, and then I add some exaggerated body language. My end result is a great caricature of a recognizable person—if I've done everything right. If not, I go back to the drawing board and start again.

In this book I will explain the process I use to carve and paint

golfing figures. You will find an extensive step-by-step project on a fellow I've named Rise and Shine. He has just rolled out of bed and onto the golf course. With a cup of coffee in one hand and a club in the other, he is ready to tackle an early morning round of golf. My goal in this demonstration is to show you the basics of how to carve, paint and finish a caricature golfer.

In addition, you will find 11 more patterns for other golfing caricatures that I've designed over the years. Some of these patterns are

challenging. Beginning caricature carvers will want to work through the demonstration first to develop the basic skills before moving on to these patterns. More experienced caricature carvers are welcome to start with any pattern that intrigues them.

As you become more experienced, don't be afraid to alter these patterns. I've included some information about armatures to aid you in developing your own patterns. An armature is a wire frame covered in clay. Bending and posing an armature will help you to ensure that your original creations are evenly balanced and anatomically correct.

Tools and Materials

I use a variety of knives and palm gouges when I carve. While I find it convenient to be able to choose from this array of tools, you, on the other hand, do not need to go out and purchase every carving instrument you see in this book. The beauty of caricature carving is that most of it can be done with a few small millimeter tools, such as v-tools, u-gouges, veiners, and a good quality detail knife.

Just as important as the carving tools are the measuring tools. You will need a ruler and a pencil to accurately mark the wood to be removed.

Painting

When you are finished carving a piece, wash it thoroughly. I suggest filling a small glass with warm water and adding just a couple drops of dishwashing liquid. Use a small brush to wash the carving then rinse it with clean, warm water. Do not soak the carving in water. Pat the carving dry with a paper towel, then set it aside to dry overnight.

I use acrylic paints to paint all of my caricature golfers. I like the fast drying time and the variety of colors. Most of the paints are thinned slightly with water. White is applied straight from the bottle on teeth and eyeballs. I apply the paints directly to the wood. I have found that sealers are unnecessary for my use.

Antiquing

Antiquing is a way to mute the colors and give them all the same tone. It is a technique commonly used by caricature carvers. The antiquing process can begin as soon as the acrylic paints are dry.

First I spray the entire carving with a matte finish to seal and protect the paint. Then I make an antiquing mixture of oil paint, boiled linseed oil and mineral spirits. (The recipe is above.) Next I apply this mixture liberally to the carving and wipe off any excess with a lint-free cloth. Finally I spray the dry carving with one last coat of matte spray finish.

Note that the rags and cloths you use to wipe away the excess antiquing mixture are flammable. Discard them safely and according to the local ordinances in your area.

Added Extras

Use your imagination to add finishing touches to your carving. Here are some of the things you'll notice on the carvings in this book:

• Carved golf balls: Create these from a small twig of birch.
• Golf clubs: Carve clubs from a forked branch. Simply remove the bark, even out the branch for the shaft, then round the other branch for the wood, iron, putter, wedge, etc.

Antiquing Mixture

1/4 tsp	linseed oil boiled
1/4"	long chunk of raw umber or Van Dyck brown oil paint straight from the tube
1 T	mineral spirits or turpentine

Put all ingredients into a small glass jar. Mix well. The consistency of the mixture should resemble mud: not too thick, but not too runny. Antiquing mixture can be stored in a sealed jar indefinitely. Increase or decrease the proportions to make more or less of the mix.

• Glasses: Twist copper wire around a pencil and then bend it around the golfer's face.
• Spikes: Cut small pieces of wire and push them firmly into the painted soles of the shoes. There is usually no need for glue as the ragged edge of the wire holds the spike in place.
• Bases: Bases can be cut from a variety of materials or purchased separately. Take note that a golfer with spiked shoes should never be placed directly on any surface that could be scratched by the spikes.
• Grass: Line the top of the base with green burlap to simulate grass.
• Mounting: Drill a hole in the base and a corresponding hole in the golfer's shoe. Insert a dowel to connect the two. The golfer can now be easily removed and replaced.

A fancy paint mixing tray is not necessary. I often mix my paints in an old egg carton or in the caps of the paints.

VARIOUS EXPRESSIONS

MADE IT!
NICE SHOT!
YES!

I DON'T KNOW WHERE
IT WENT...

HOW COULD I MISS
THAT ONE?

HOW'D I MISS THAT ONE?

NOTHIN TO IT!

THAT'S THE 3RD SHOT
IN THE LAKE.

HEY! THAT'S MY BALL!

IT'S IN THE OTHER
FAIRWAY.

FORE!
WATCH OUT!

CLOSE!...

Bill Hourula ©
2002

THAT'S A GIMME...AIN'T IT!

NICE TRY!

HOW ON EARTH DID
I MISS THAT?

NOTHING TO IT!

I SAW THAT LOIS!

THIS IS SOO FUN!

THAT WAS SO CLOSE
I COULD SCREAM.

I PUT SOME POWDER
ON THAT DRIVE.

I TOOK A NINE ON
THAT LAST HOLE.

I'M DA MAN!

OH BOY!

Bill Hourula ©
2002

Making and Using an Armature

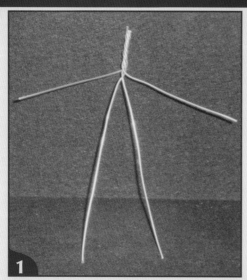

To make an armature, twist four pieces of #14 copper wire together.

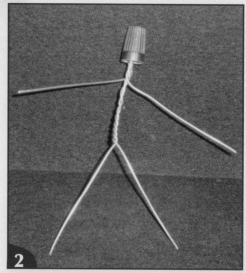

Twist an electrical wire nut on top to resemble the head and twist the two bottom wires to form the body and the legs.

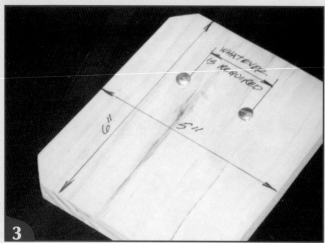

Create a base for the armature from 3/4" thick wood. Two 5/8" long sheet metal screws are placed a specified distance apart for the feet.

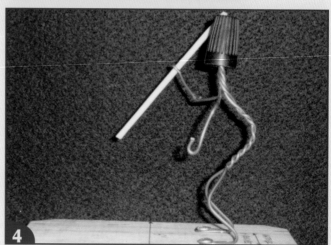

Bend the ends of the bottom two wires so they can be attached to a base. You now have a flexible figure with which you can experiment and perfect different poses.

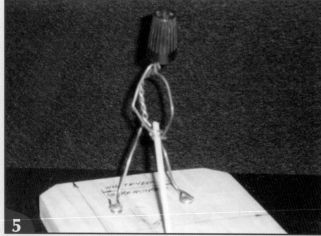

A stick forms a simple golf club that can be positioned accordingly.

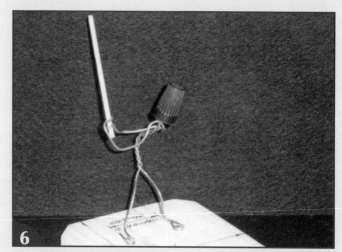

As you move the figure, be sure to move the entire body to accommodate a full range of motion.

PART TWO

CARVING A GOLFER STEP-BY-STEP

In the following demonstration I use a previously carved figure as a guide. I've included several "comparison shots" that show you the in-progress carving alongside the finished figure. Keep this direct comparison in mind as you are carving, and you will find that you will have a better grasp of the overall carving process. In lieu of a finished carving, you can use the final project shots at the end of this chapter as reference.

Also, note that I don't carve one small area to completion before moving on to the next. Like most caricature carvers, I work around the entire piece, making adjustments as I go to ensure the overall appeal of the finished piece.

Let's get started. I'm using a block of basswood, approximately 2" x 2" x 4" in this demonstration.

Rise and Shine
© Bill Howrilla

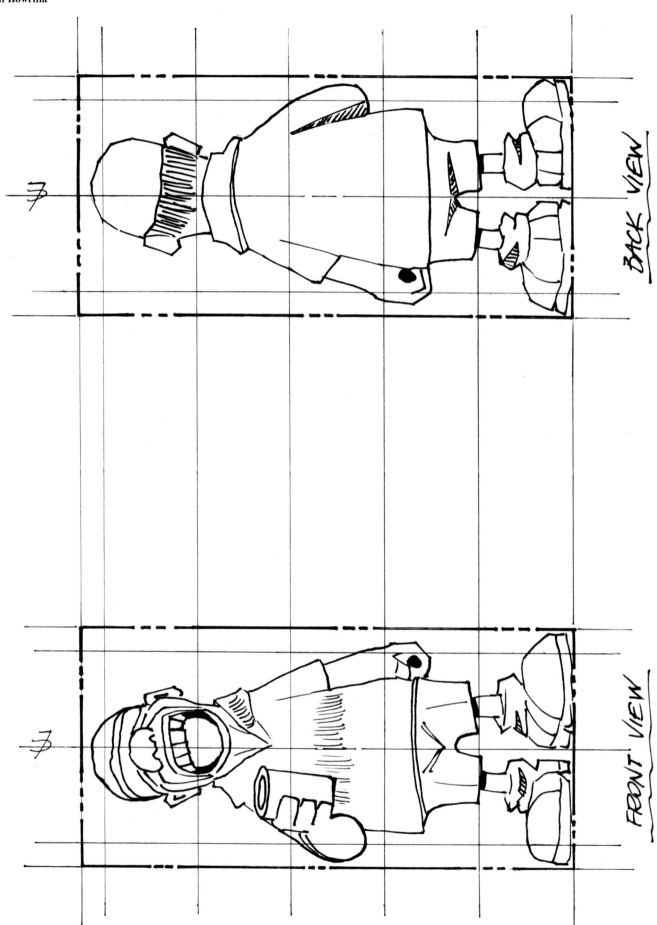

BACK VIEW

FRONT VIEW

Rise and Shine

© Bill Howrilla

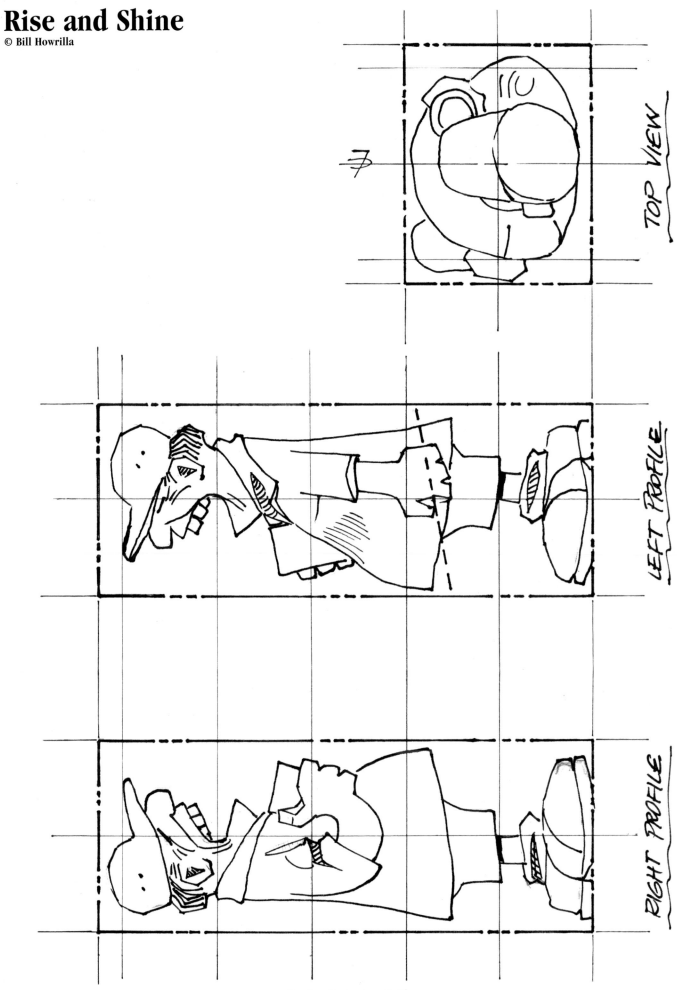

TOP VIEW

LEFT PROFILE

RIGHT PROFILE

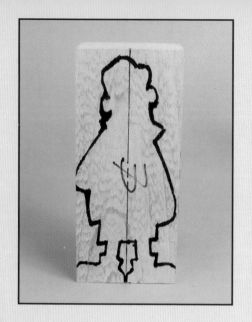

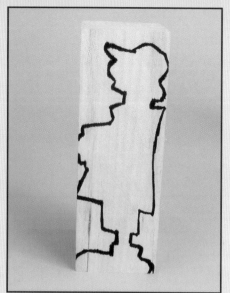

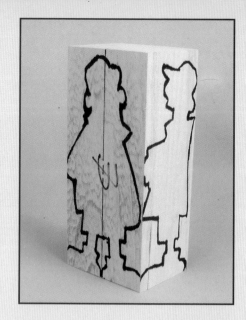

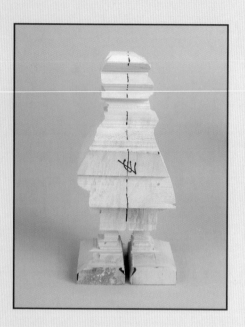

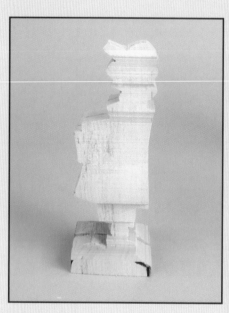

Preparing a Bandsaw Blank

Preparing a bandsaw blank is an important preliminary step. Your carving time can be dramatically decreased, depending on how you saw the blank.

First, make a template of the patterns. I usually make my templates from thick card stock. That way all I have to do is trace around the pattern I want to use and put it away for safe keeping until the next time around. Other options include making a template from plywood or acetate.

Next, trace the pattern to the block of wood. Note that the pattern shape takes into account many of the dips and turns of the finished carving's outline. Creating a bandsaw blank that is as close as possible to your finished carving is what saves time.

Finally, cut the pattern on a bandsaw. Be sure to follow the manufacturer's directions for use and safety.

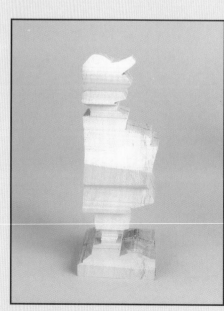

Rough Carving

1. Work begins on the golfer's head. First draw in the ear; then, outline the ear with a v-tool.

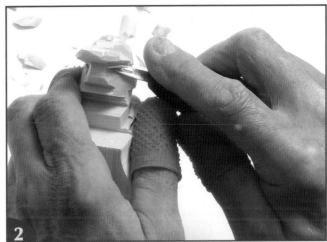

2. Make a stop cut under the brim of the hat and remove a small amount of wood up to this cut. This shallow cut is the first definition of the eye placement.

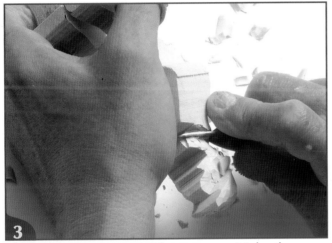

3. Define the neck area with stop cuts. Make these cuts on both sides of the carving to ensure that the cuts on both sides are even.

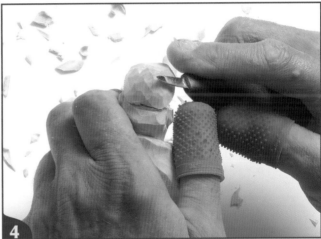

4. Round the corners of the hat with a carving knife. Work all over the hat to ensure symmetry; don't carve one side completely before moving on to the other side.

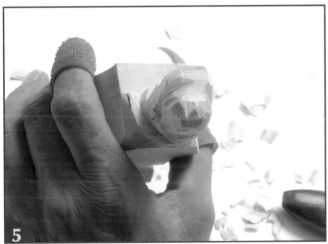

5. A view from the top shows the rounded cap to this point. Notice that the final rounding of the cap will be completed later.

6. Work continues next on the golfer's left side and back. Draw in the arm holding the club. Here I am using a finished carving as a reference. Use the finished photographs or the pattern in the same manner.

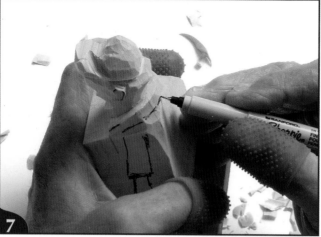

7 Draw in the back of the collar at this time as well. I usually use a pencil to draw on the wood. Here I am using a marker for photographic reasons.

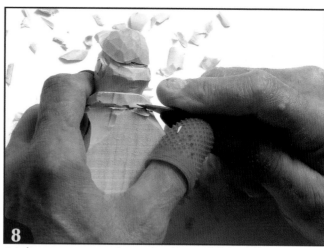

8 Make a stop cut along the line of the collar and remove wood up to this cut.

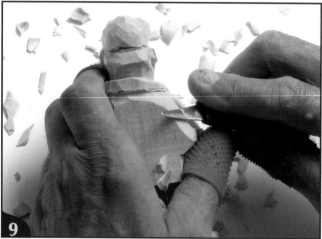

9 Knock the hard edges of the bandsaw blank off the shoulders.

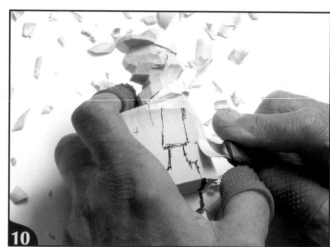

10 Turning the carving to the side, remove wood around the lines defining the arm.

11 Draw the outlines of the feet on the bottom of the blank according to the pattern and the finished photos.

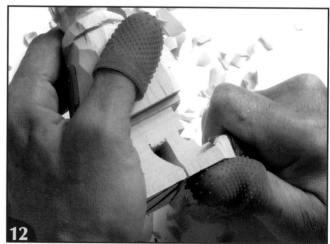

12 Knock the corners off the feet with a carving knife. These cuts block in the basic shape and make it easier to hold the carving.

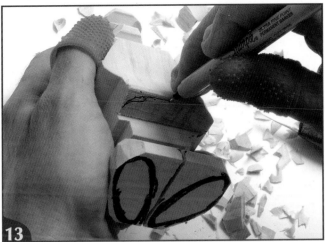

13 Draw the outline of the shirt as shown. This line will indicate how much wood to remove from this portion of the blank.

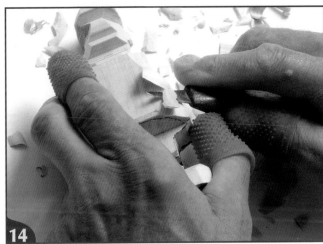

14 Using a carving knife, remove wood from the bottom of the shirt to the center of the torso as shown.

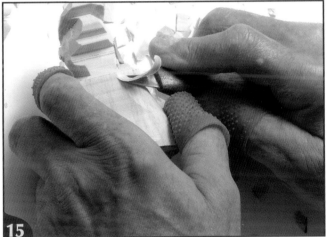

15 Remove the wood from the center of the torso to the top of the shirt.

16 With the point of the carving knife, make a stop cut along the lines of the arm.

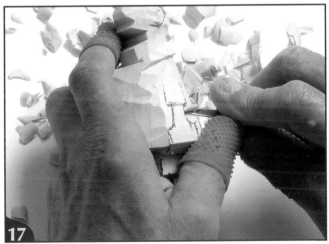

17 Remove the excess wood to the right of the stop cut with slicing cuts.

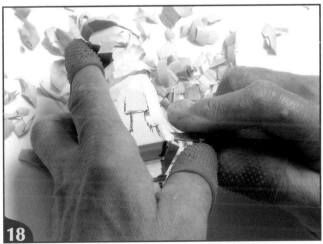

18 Continue to remove excess wood from the outside of the arm. These cuts will relieve the arm from the body.

Carve the Arms

19 On the side view draw the outline for the right arm. Use the finished photographs and the pattern as reference.

20 Continue the drawing on the front of the blank.

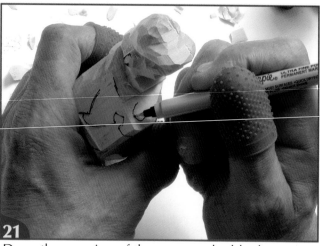

21 Draw the opening of the mug on the blank as shown.

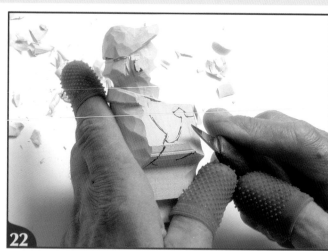

22 Begin to shape the right arm by removing the hard edges of the blank with the carving knife.

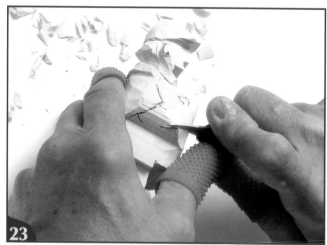

23 Make a stop cut on the line that defines the elbow.

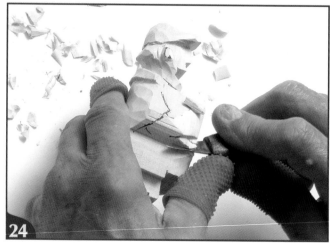

24 Remove excess wood up to this cut. You will need to make several stop cuts and several subsequent cuts to reach the required depth.

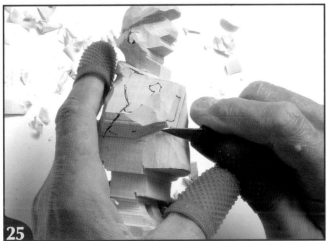

25

The final result of the cuts should look like this.

26

The same sequence of cuts is used to start roughing in the coffee mug in the golfer's right hand. First make a stop cut.

27

Then remove wood up to that cut.

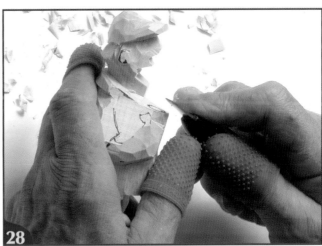

28

You may need to repeat this process several times until you reach the required depth. Be careful that you do not remove the wood that will form the golfer's hand.

29

Another stop cut marks the opposite side of the golfer's coffee mug.

30

Remove the excess wood up to this cut to make the coffee mug stand out from the body. Notice that I have switched to a more convenient knife to carve this area. A carving knife can be used here, also.

31

Make a stop cut and remove the excess wood at the bottom of the coffee mug.

32

Repeat the same process under the golfer's arm.

33

The right arm has been partially shaped at this point. Notice that I have made some additional small cuts to give some roundness to this part of the arm.

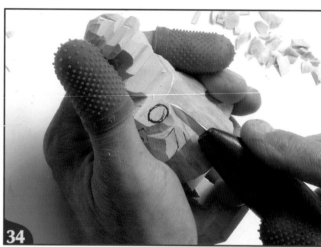

34

Clean up the area where the coffee mug meets the golfer's shirt.

35

Draw the golfer's fingers and round the mug. Start now to make some of the small cuts that shape the front of the golfer's shirt.

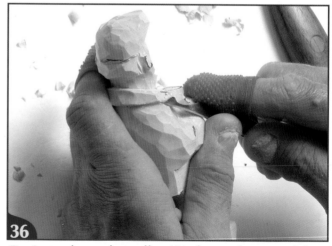

36

Begin to shape the collar. Work evenly around the entire figure, removing small amounts of wood as you carve.

37 The top of the collar should be a flat plane. I have switched back to a regular carving knife to make these cuts.

38 Using a u-gouge with the same shape as the curvature of the mug, cut the lines that define the inside of the mug.

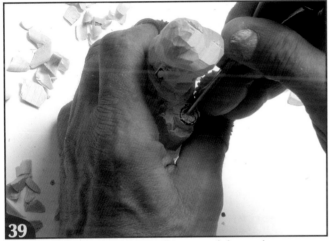

39 With small cuts, remove the wood from the center of the mug. Do not apply too much pressure on the outside edge of the mug; it may break. The center of the mug can also be drilled out very slowly with a Forstner bit.

40 Remove excess wood from the crook of the golfer's elbow with a carving knife or a small gouge. Here I am using a gouge.

41 Continue to shape the golfer's arm with a carving knife.

42 Use the carving knife to make v-cuts to separate the golfer's fingers.

43 Shape the underside of the arm by making stop cuts and removing wood from the body above and below the elbow.

44 Round and shape the back of the arm. Continue shaping the rest of the arm before you move on to the next step.

Carve the Face and Head

46 Carving the face is next. Remember to refer often to the photos of the finished piece and to the pattern as you carve.

45 Using the gouge and the carving knife, outline, rough-in and shape the left arm.

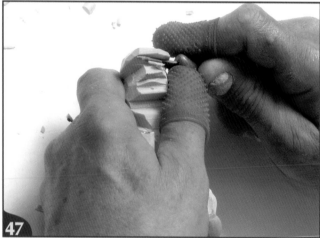

47 Using a carving knife, remove wood from under the bill of the cap. Don't push up on the bill as you carve; it may break.

48 A gouge will help you to remove wood from the concave area under the bill.

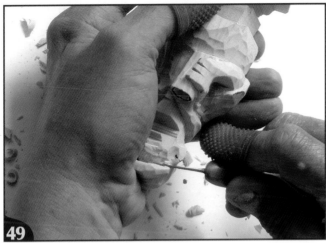

49

Begin to shape the face. Make small cuts with the knife. Refer often to the finished photos and carve evenly all over the face.

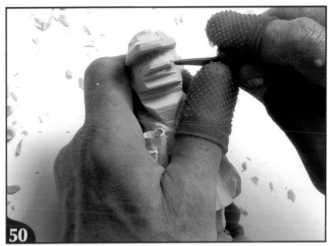

50

Cut in the corner of the nose.

51

The cut should look like this.

52

When both sides of the nose are cut, it's time to work on the mouth. Draw the smile lines on both sides of the nose as shown.

53

Cut in the smile lines with a v-tool. You may need to turn the piece upside-down to complete this step.

54

Remove a small amount of wood from the surface of the teeth, making them stand out from the lips.

55

The mouth should look like this at this stage. Notice that it is not perfectly symmetrical.

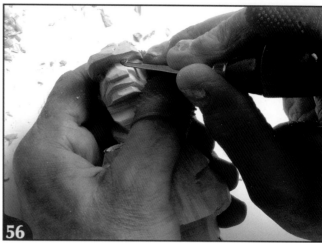

56

Use a u-gouge to hollow out the eye sockets. These cuts are made right under the hat brim.

57

The interior of the mouth is carved next. Draw the lines that separate the teeth and the line that marks the inside of the lower lip as shown.

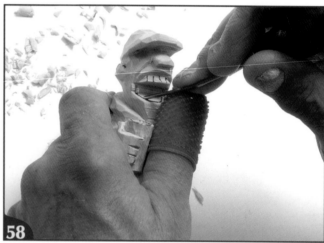

58

Carve along the line that marks the inside of the lower lip with a small v-tool or veiner.

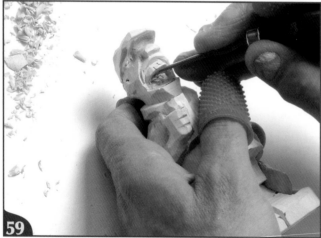

59

Continuing to use the u-gouge, carve away the wood on the roof of the mouth to create a concave area behind the teeth.

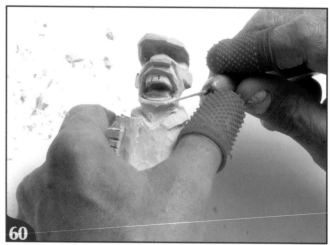

60

Remove the wood under the chin on both sides of the neck. These cuts will narrow the neck and help to create the golfer's jaw line.

61

Use a small gouge to widen the line that separates the tongue from the lower lip.

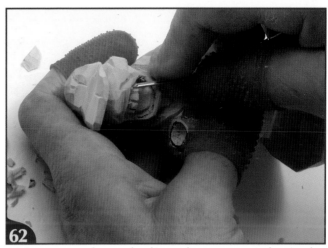

62

Using a v-tool, cut the lines that separate the teeth.

63

Draw the lines that define the inner ear. These lines make a triangular shape.

64

Push the knife tip in at an angle along the lines.

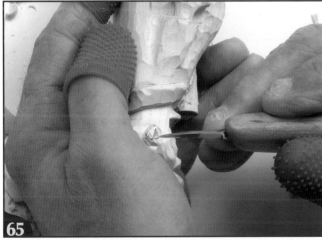

65

When you cut the third side of the triangle, a chip should pop out.

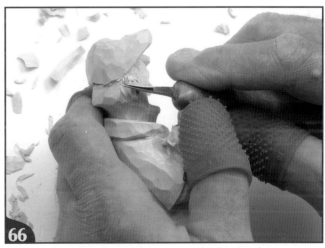

66

Shape the outside of the ear with the knife. Use a small veiner in the back of the ear.

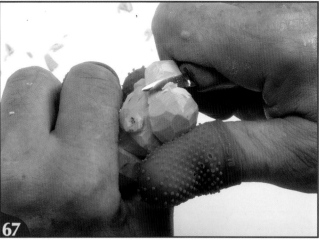

67 Use the knife to remove wood from the crown of the hat and from the bill of the hat. In this photo, you can also see the final shape of the ear.

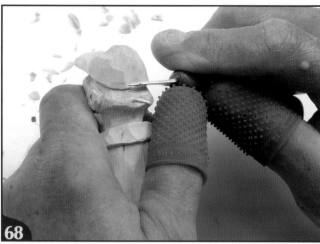

68 Make the cut between the hat and the hair deeper to better define the area where the hat meets the hair.

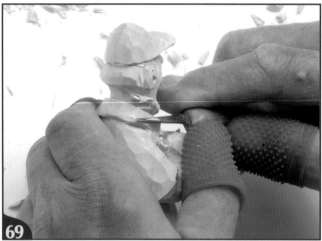

69 Remove wood from the back of the neck and clean up the collar as you go. These cuts will make the neck narrower.

70 Simulate hair with a v-tool. These cuts should not be evenly spaced.

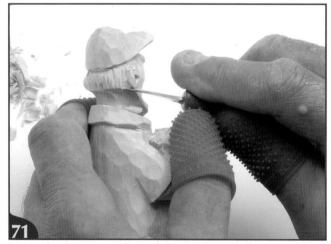

71 Trim the bottom edge of the hair and clean up the neck as you go.

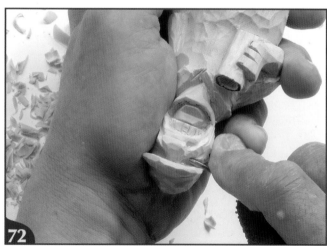

72 Finalize the space for the eyes with the u-gouge. Study the photographs of the finished piece to ensure the proper placement and depth.

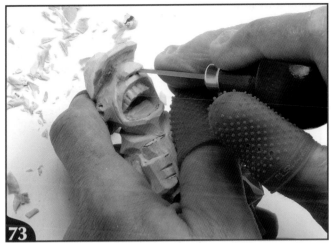

73 Draw the nostrils under the nose and remove the wood with a u-gouge.

74 Do some overall cleanup work on the coat. Sharpen the ridge where the collar meets the shirt, define the v-neck, add some creases in the crook of the elbow, and shape the back.

75 Mark the lines that separate the fingers of the left hand.

76 Use the u-gouge to define the separation between the arm and the shirt. Also carve the lines that separate the fingers at this time.

Carve the Legs and Feet

77 Remove the large chunk of wood between the golfer's feet in several cuts.

78 Continue to remove wood from the sides, tops and backs of the shoes until you have the desired shape.

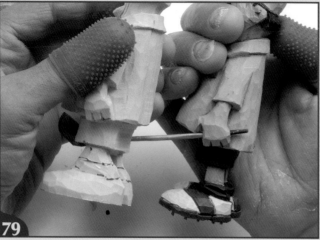

79
Draw the socks.

80
Remove wood from the legs and carve the wrinkles in the socks. Remove wood a little bit at a time through a series of stop cuts.

81
Draw the lines that define the crotch and the legs on the front of the golfer's pants.

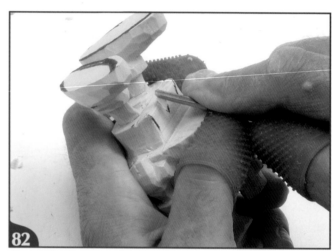

82
Remove the wood from the crotch of the pants with a small u-gouge or detail knife.

83
Clean up the area with a specialty knife or a carving knife.

84
Draw the lines that define the crotch and the legs on the back of the golfer's pants.

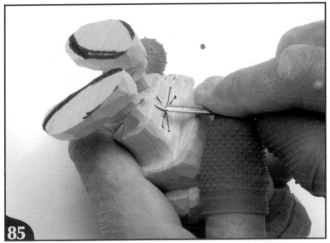

85

Cut these lines with a u-gouge or detail knife, which can also be used to make creases in the pants.

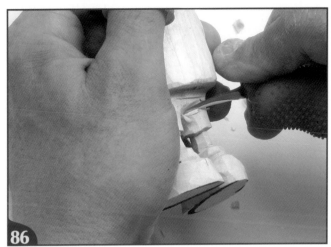

86

Clean up the area with a carving knife.

87

Even though the bottoms of the shoes are not readily visible, they still need to be carved. Mark the lines showing the heel on both shoes.

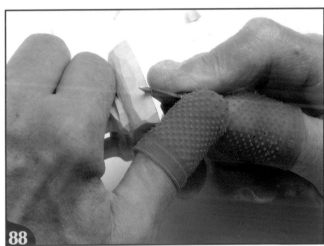

88

Make the first angled cut of a v-cut with a detail knife as shown.

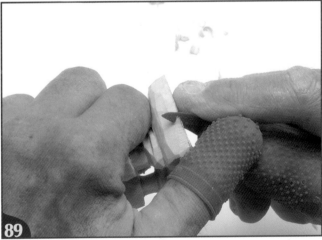

89

Make a second cut as shown to remove a wedge of wood.

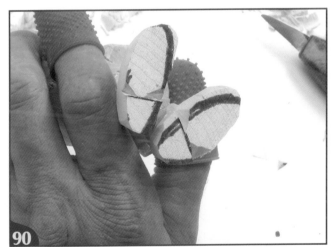

90

Repeat these cuts on the insides and outside of both shoes.

91

Give the toes of the shoes a slight lift by carving away a small amount of wood from the front of the soles. In this photo, the shoe on the left is finished.

92

Mark the lines that separate the soles of the shoes from the leather uppers. Also separate the colored sections as shown.

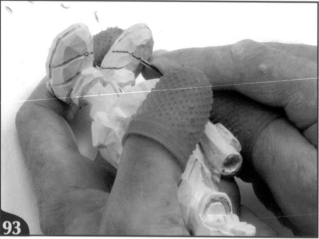

93

Carve all the lines with a small v-tool or a series of stop cuts for any desired details.

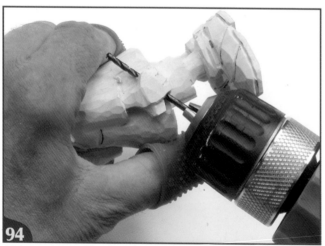

94

When the golfer has been carved to your satisfaction, drill the hole for the club slowly, making sure you don't break the hand.

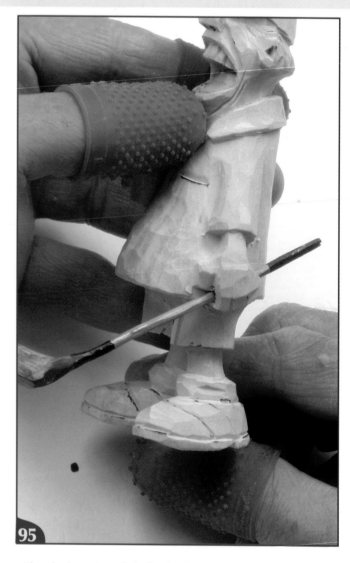

95

Check that the club fits before moving on to the next step. Do not glue it in place yet.

Painting Guide

Use watered-down acrylic paints to paint the golfer. (See the section on painting in the Introduction for more information on how to thin your paints.) The colors here are just suggestions. Acrylic paints dry fast. Paint in the order shown here, but be sure to allow one area to dry before you move on to the next.

Teeth: White

Lips and inside of mouth: Pink

Face: Flesh

Hair: Black

Cap: Tan

Mug: White

Legs: Flesh

Shoes: White and black

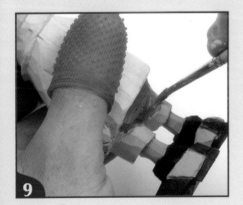

Pants: Gray

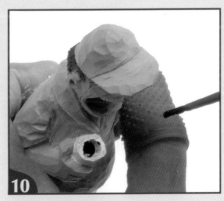

Coffee: Black

Shirt: Yellow

Finishing Techniques

Mount the figure on a stylus and spray it lightly with sealer.

Paint the top half of the figure liberally with antiquing medium.

Rub off any excess antiquing medium immediately with a soft cloth.

Repeat this process on the lower half of the figure.

This golfer is now ready for his 5 a.m. tee time.

PART THREE
PATTERN GALLERY

Judging the Distance

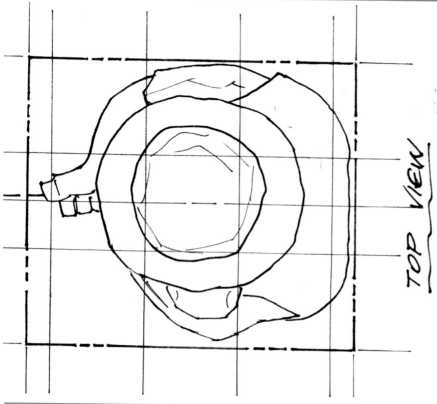

TOP VIEW

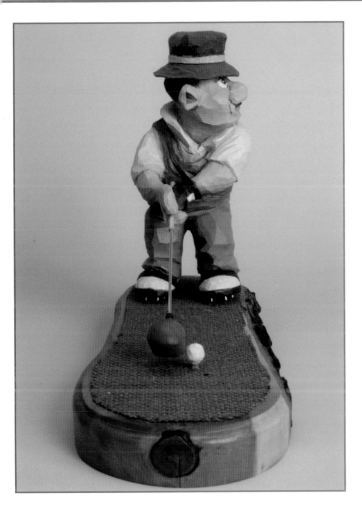

Judging the Distance
© Bill Howrilla

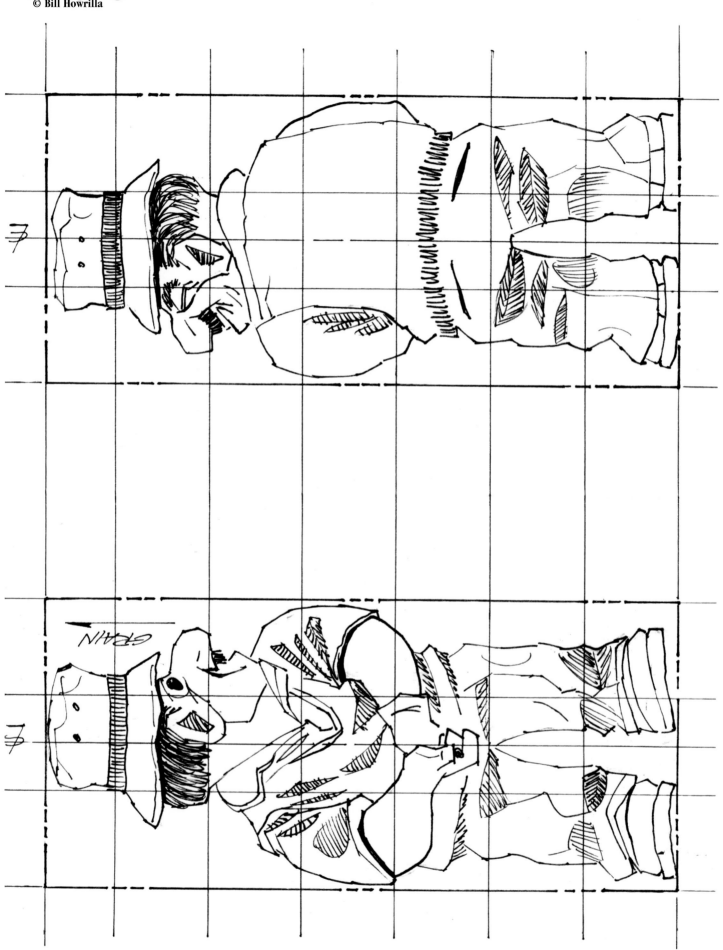

Carving Caricature Golfers

Judging the Distance
© Bill Howrilla

LEFT PROFILE

RIGHT PROFILE

GRAIN

Perfect Form

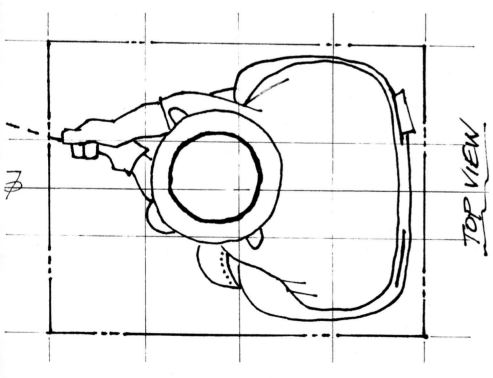

TOP VIEW

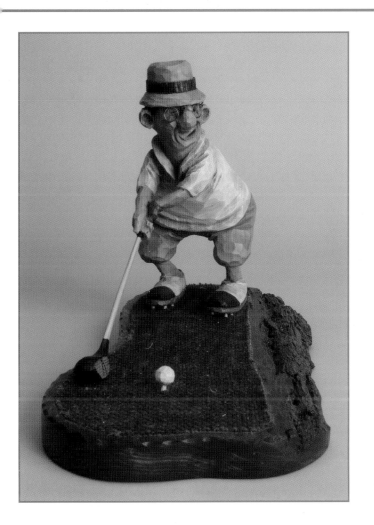

Perfect Form
© Bill Howrilla

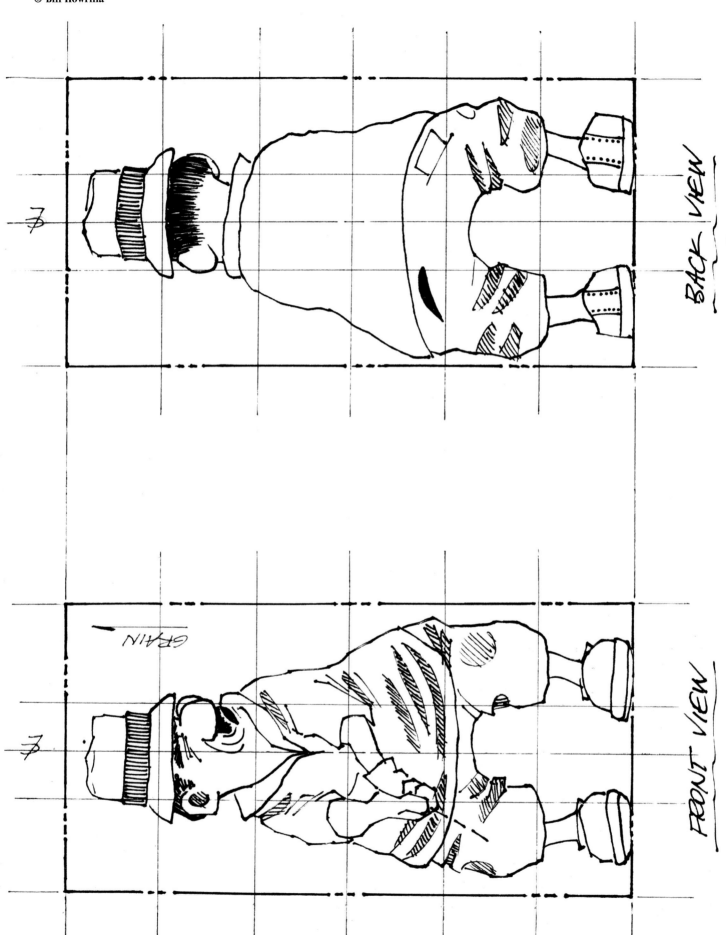

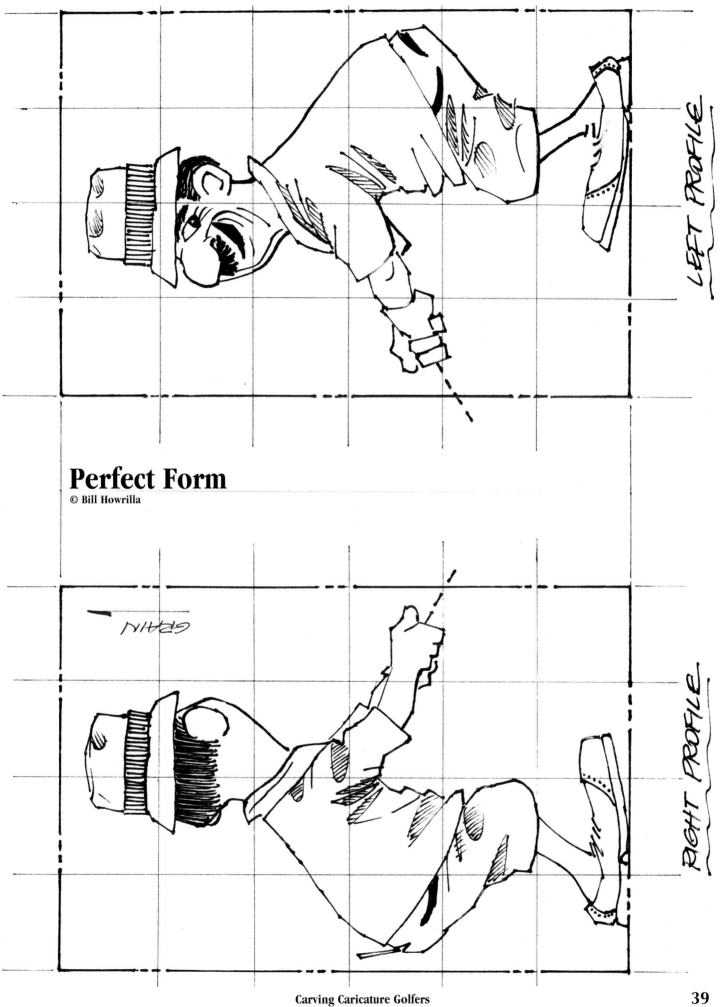

Perfect Form

© Bill Howrilla

LEFT PROFILE

RIGHT PROFILE

GRAIN

Concentration

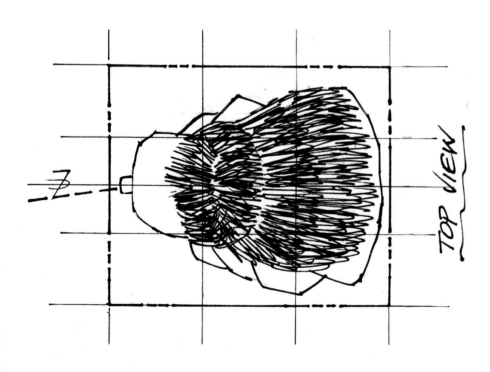

TOP VIEW

Concentration
© Bill Howrilla

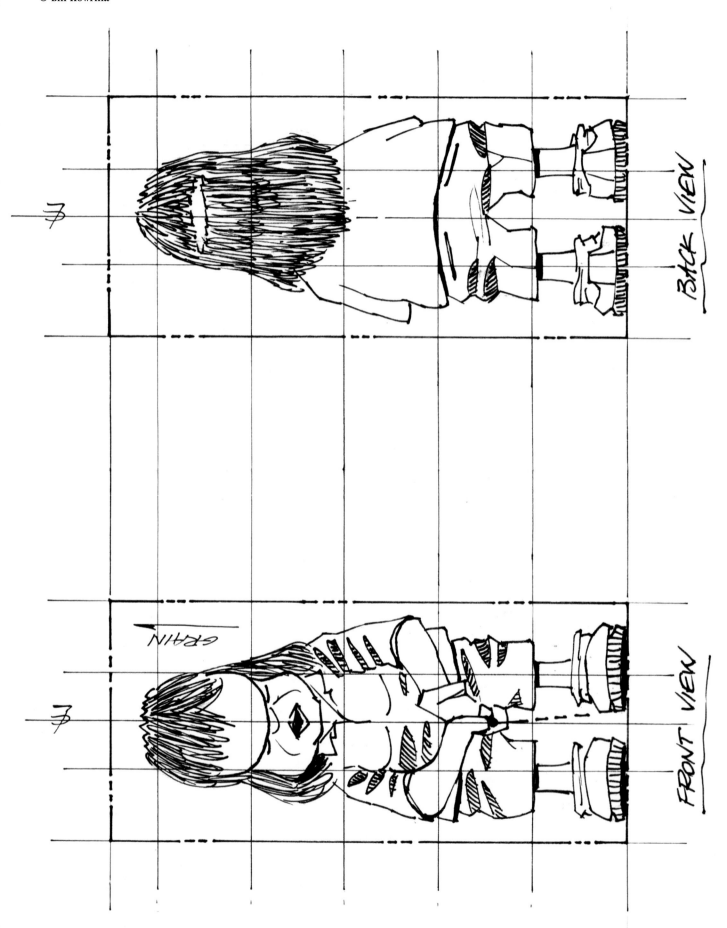

Concentration
© Bill Howrilla

LEFT PROFILE

RIGHT PROFILE

GRAIN

No Sweat

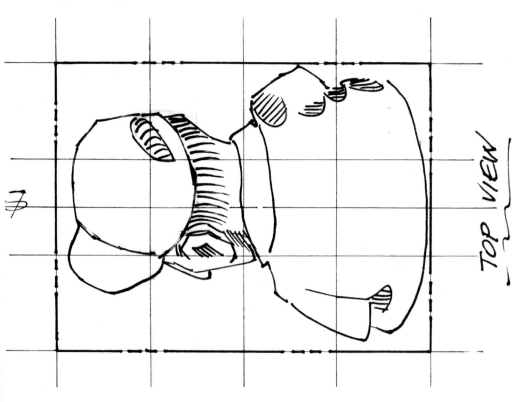

TOP VIEW

No Sweat
© Bill Howrilla

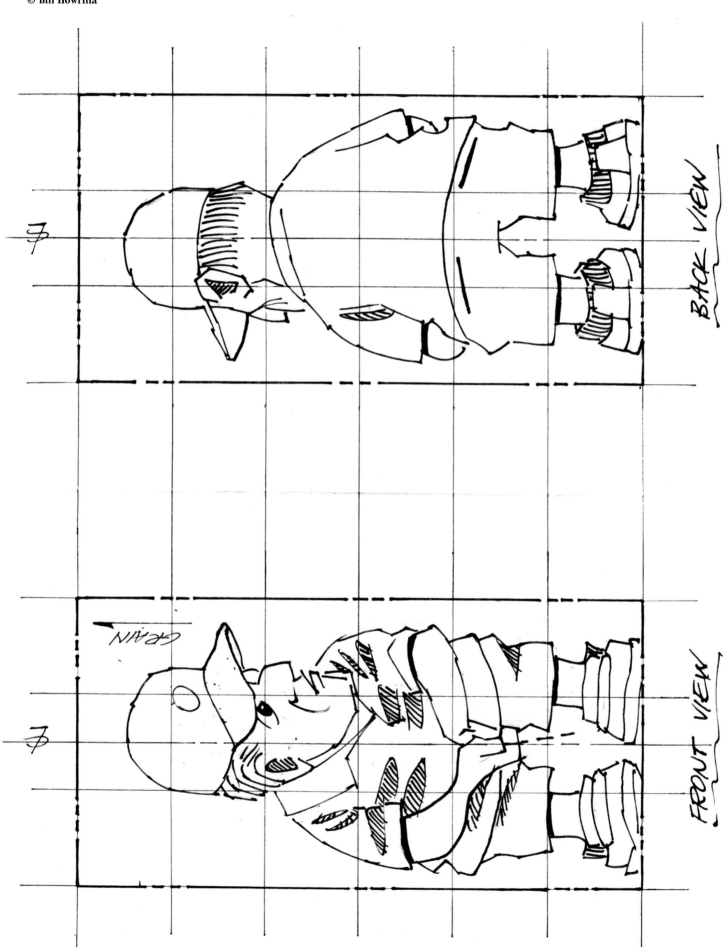

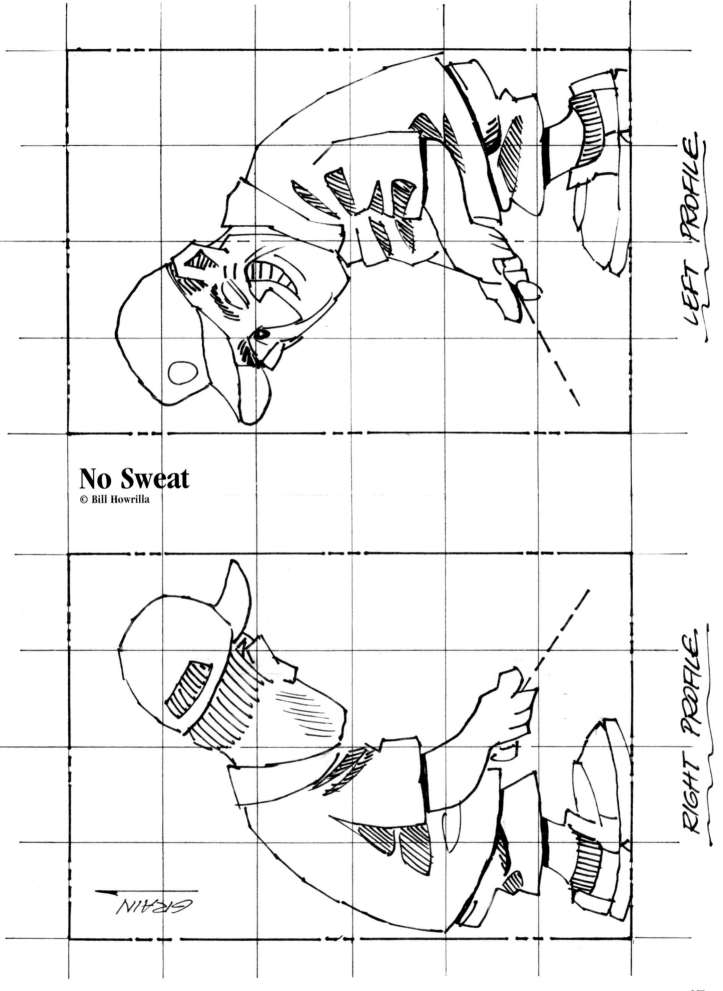

No Sweat
© Bill Howrilla

LEFT PROFILE

RIGHT PROFILE

GRAIN

Geez!

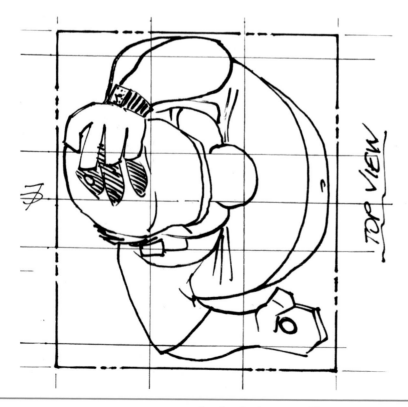

TOP VIEW

Geez!

© Bill Howrilla

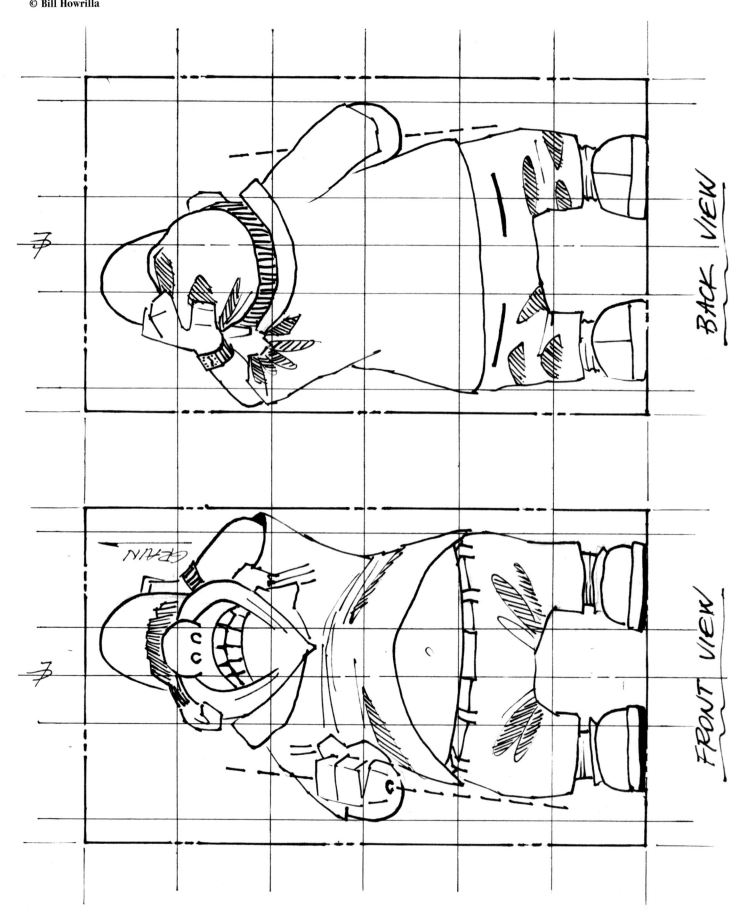

Geez!
© Bill Howrilla

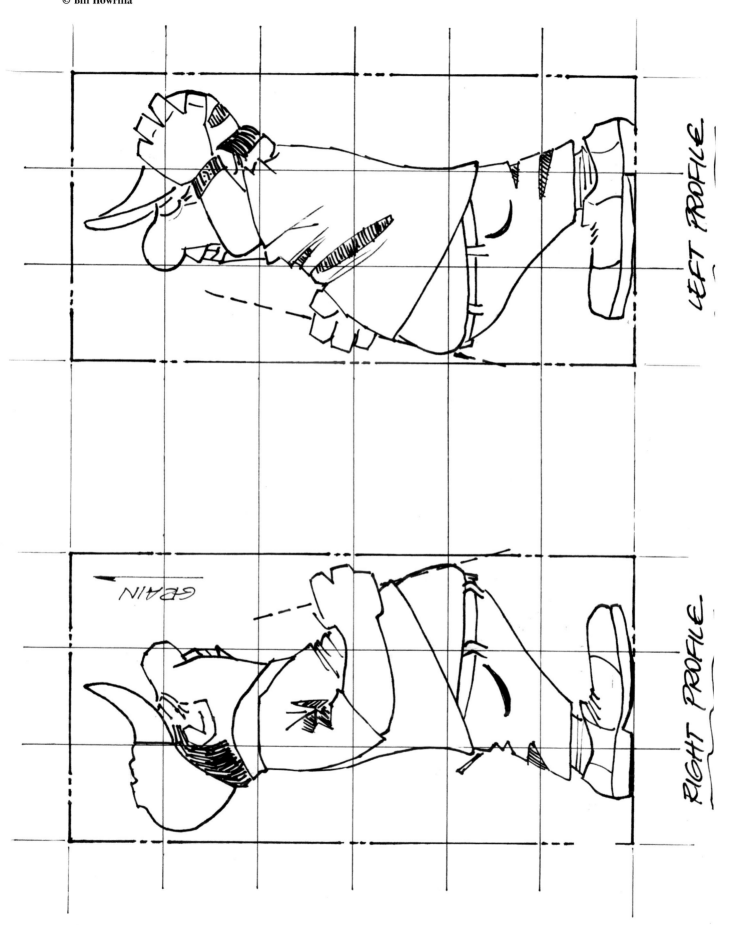

LEFT PROFILE

RIGHT PROFILE

GRAIN

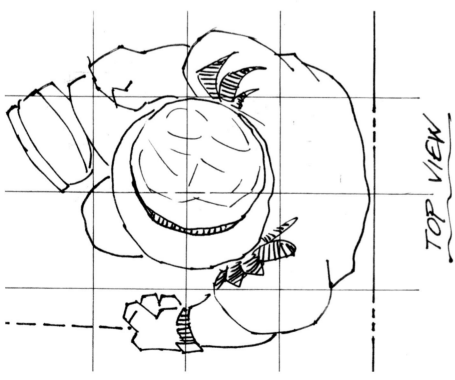

TOP VIEW

Yes!
© Bill Howrilla

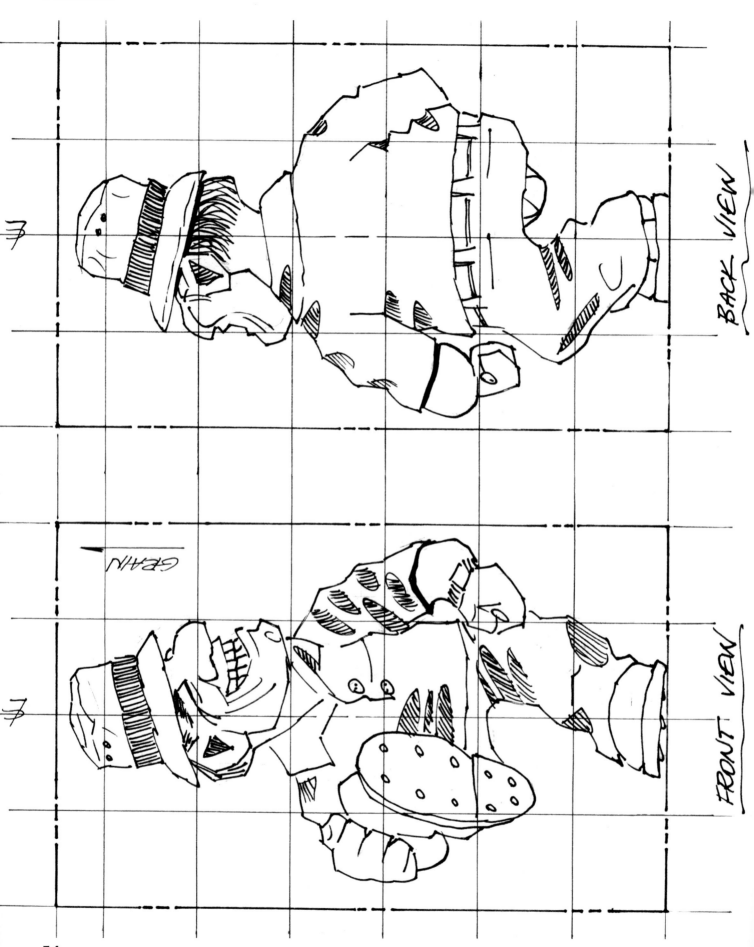

Carving Caricature Golfers

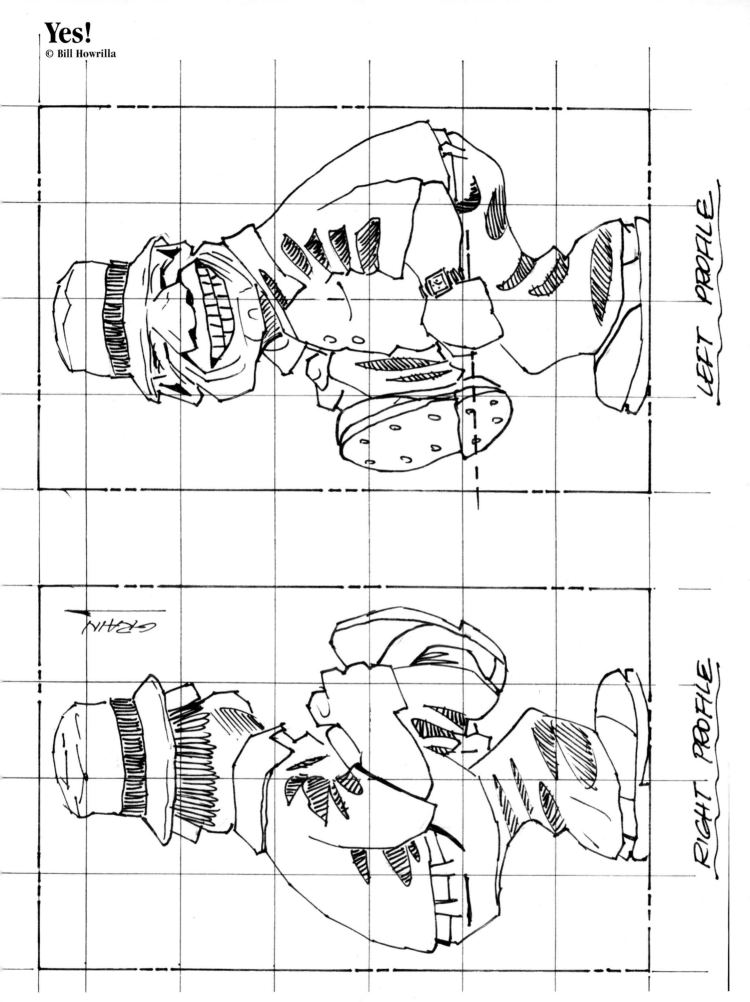

LEFT PROFILE

RIGHT PROFILE

GRAIN

What the . . . ?!

© Bill Howrilla

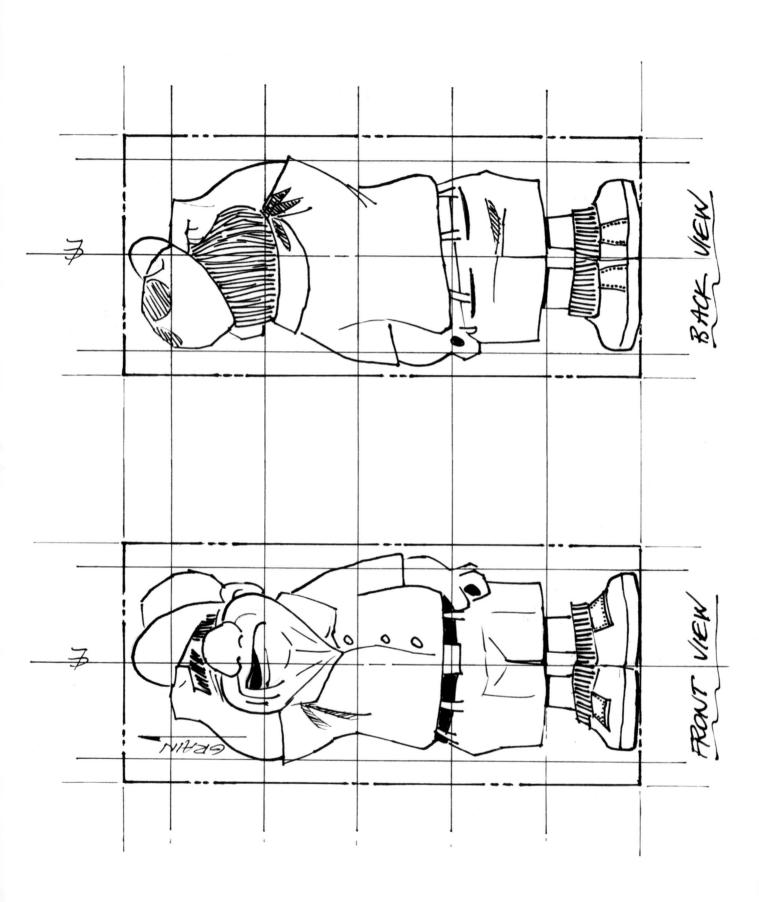

What the . . . ?!
© Bill Howrilla

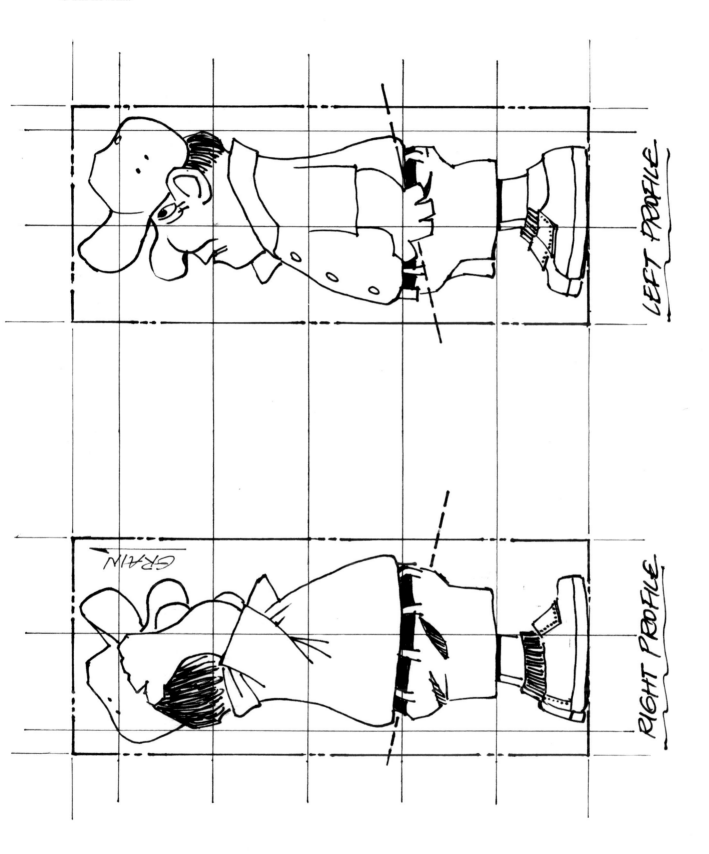

LEFT PROFILE

GRAIN

RIGHT PROFILE

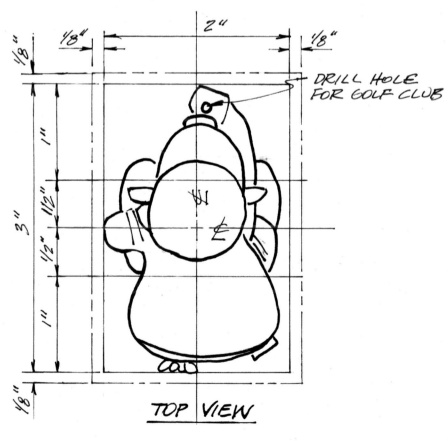

DRILL HOLE
FOR GOLF CLUB

TOP VIEW

2"

1/8"

1/8"

1/8"

1"

1/2"

1/2"

3"

1"

1/8"

Lining It Up

© Bill Howrilla

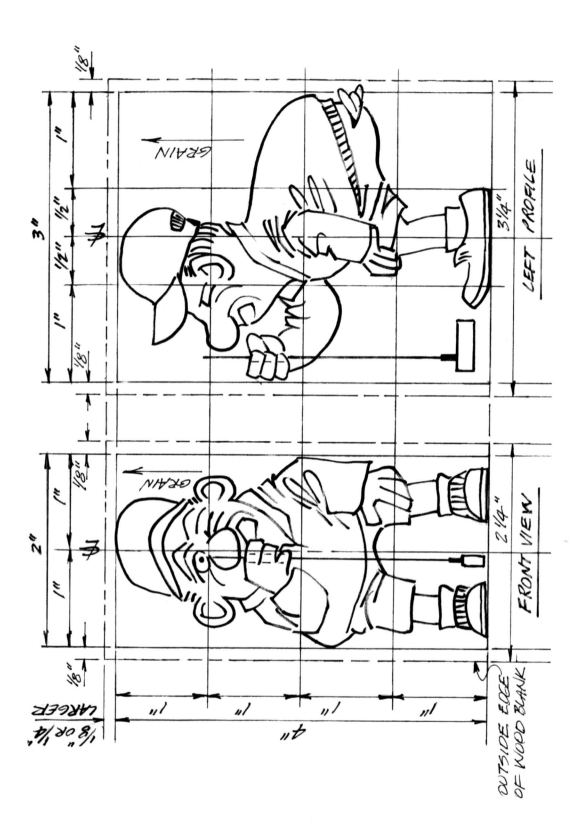

Lining It Up
© Bill Howrilla

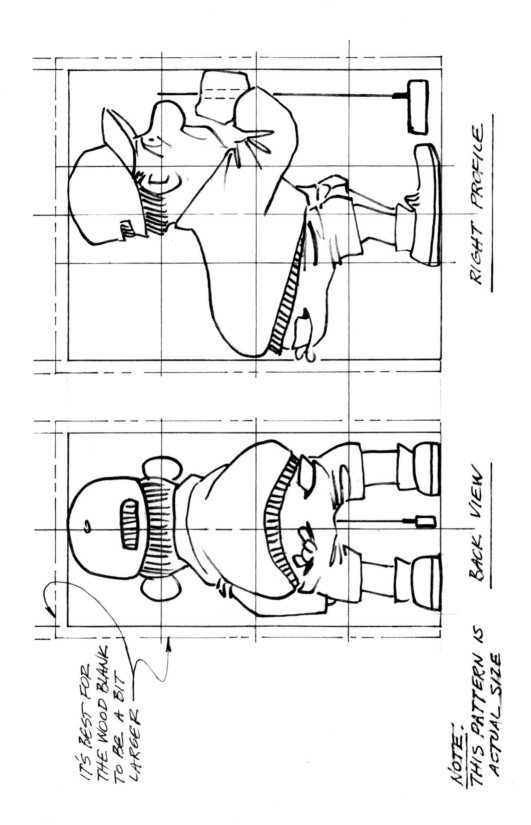

RIGHT PROFILE

BACK VIEW

IT'S BEST FOR THE WOOD BLANK TO BE A BIT LARGER

NOTE: THIS PATTERN IS ACTUAL SIZE

No Way
© Bill Howrilla

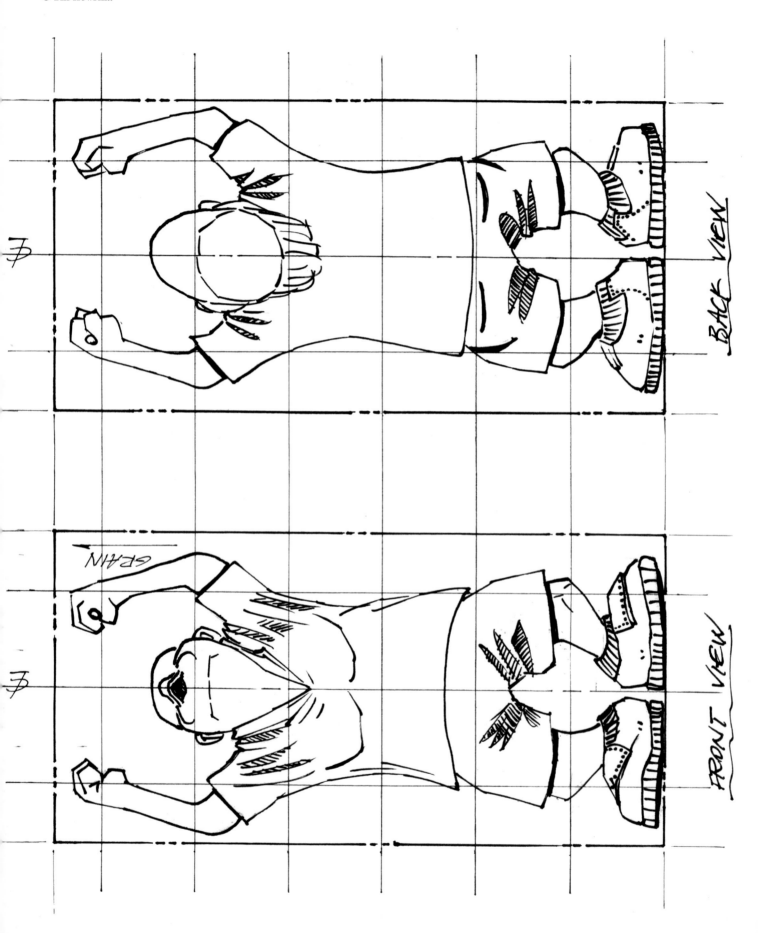

BACK VIEW

FRONT VIEW

No Way
© Bill Howrilla

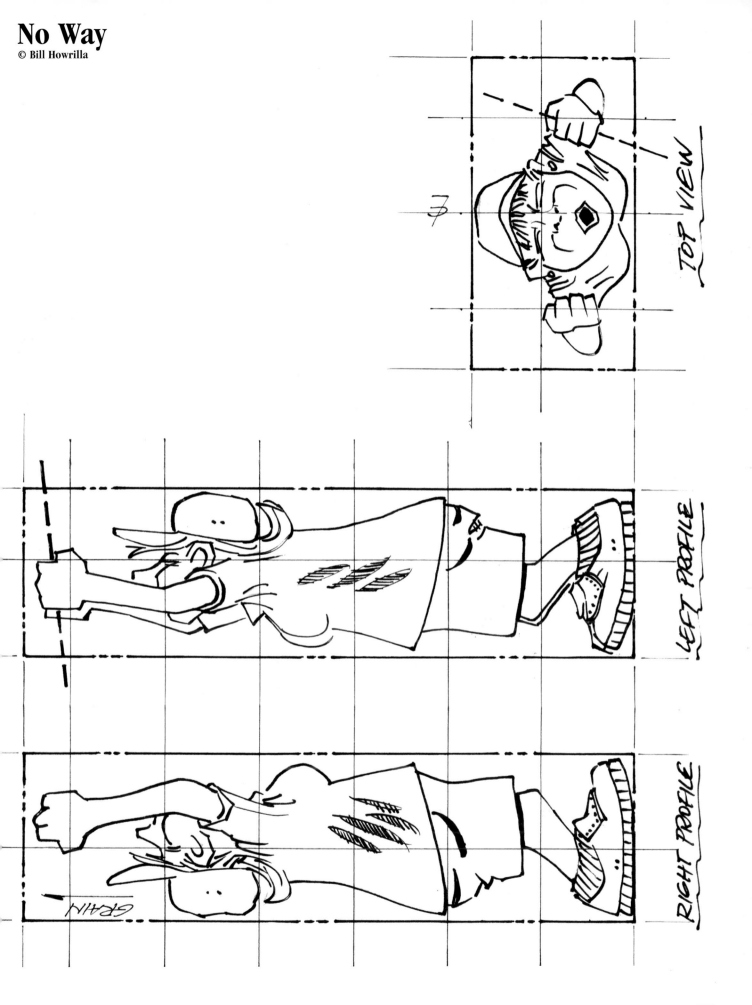

TOP VIEW

LEFT PROFILE

RIGHT PROFILE

GRAIN

Please Oh Please

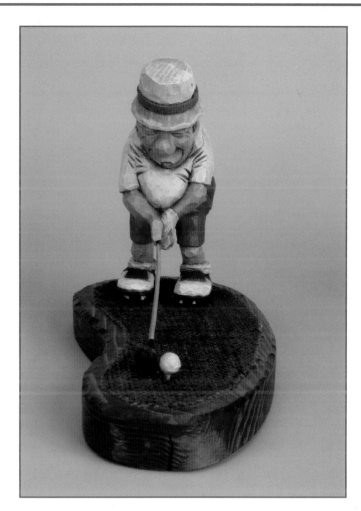

Please Oh Please

© Bill Howrilla

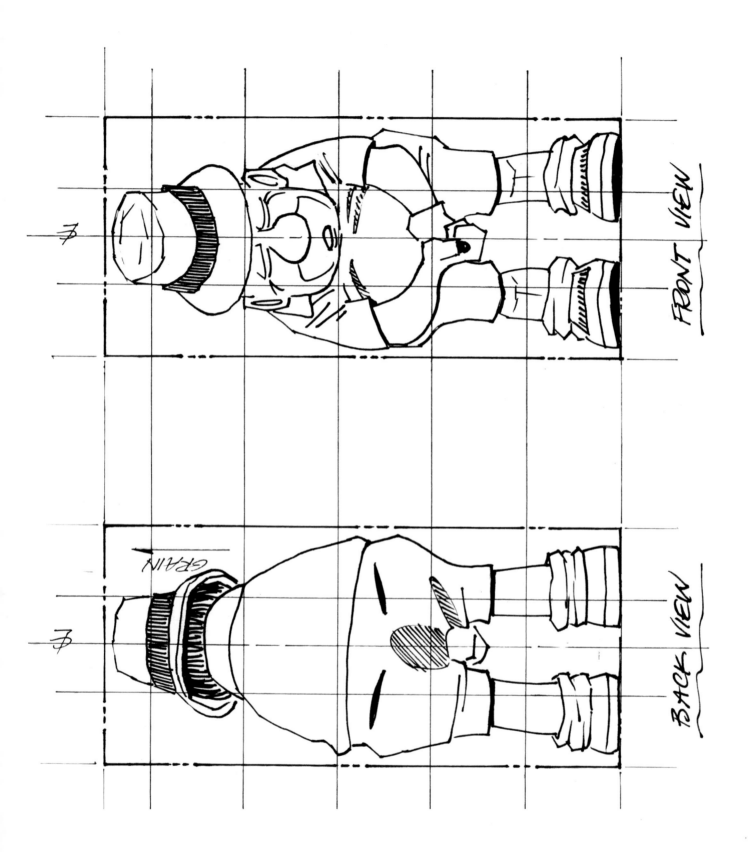

FRONT VIEW

BACK VIEW

GRAIN

Please Oh Please
© Bill Howrilla

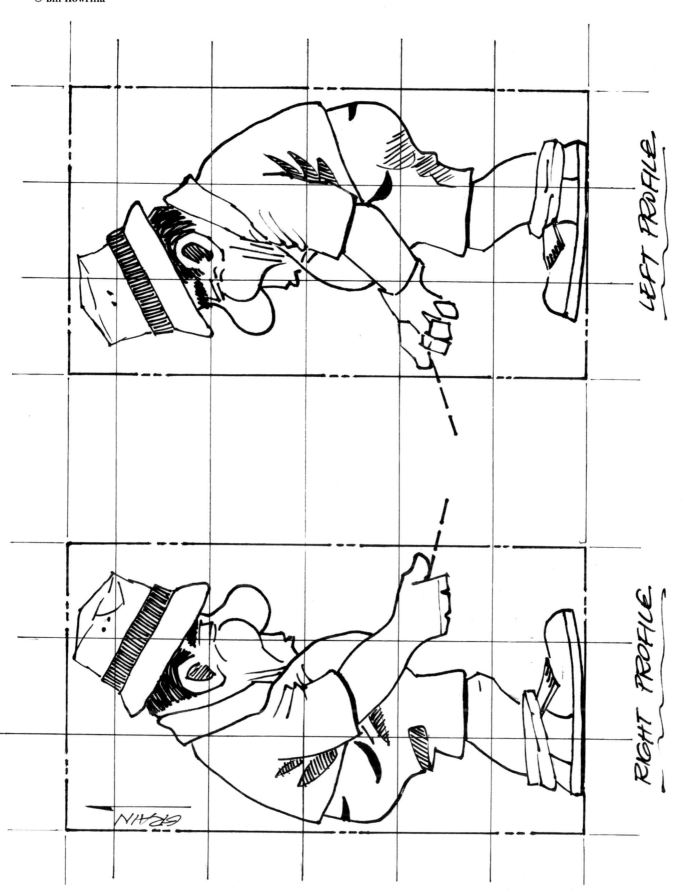

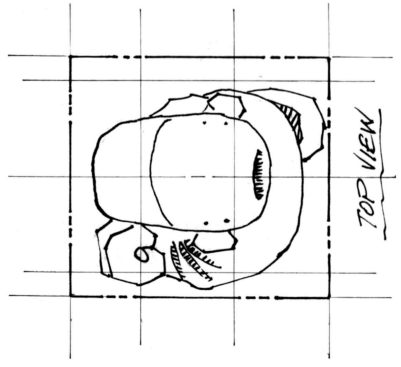

TOP VIEW

On Par
© Bill Howrilla

LEFT PROFILE

RIGHT PROFILE

On Par
© Bill Howrilla

BACK VIEW

FRONT VIEW

GRAIN

More Great Project Books from Fox Chapel Publishing

- **Woodcarving the Country Bear by Mike Shipley:** Not quite caricature, but not realistic, these humorous creatures are easy and enjoyable to carve. The book features 12 woodland creatures, including a bear and a moose, step-by-step instructions and easy-to-use patterns. A complete carving and painting project will teach you all the techniques you'll need to know to finish the other projects in the book.
ISBN: 1-56523-211-9, 64 pages, soft cover, $12.95.

- **Caricature Carving from Head to Toe by Dave Stetson:** Find out what makes a carving "caricature" with this top-notch guide from Dave Stetson. First you will learn how anatomy relates to expression by creating a clay mold. Then, you will follow the author step-by-step through an entire carving project for an Old Man with Walking Stick. Additional patterns for alternate facial expressions, overview of wood selection, tools, and an expansive photo gallery also included.
ISBN: 1-56523-121-x, 96 pages, soft cover, $19.95.

- **Complete Beginners Woodcarving Workbook 2nd Edition by Mary Duke Guldan:** Any hobbyist new to the art of woodcarving will appreciate the easy-to-follow tone of this "made for beginners" book. Special chapter on carving miniature jointed dolls and teddy bears included!
ISBN: 1-56523-197-X, 64 pages, soft cover, $9.95.

- **Whittling Twigs and Branches by Chris Lubkemann:** A knife and a little know-how is all you need to turn simple twigs into miniature wonders! Learn basic curling techniques required to create flowers, roosters and more. Perfect for beginning and experienced whittlers!
ISBN: 1-56523-149-X, 64 pages, soft cover, $9.95.

- **Extreme Pumpkin Carving by Vic Hood and Jack Williams:** A new twist on classic holiday tradition: Learn to carve three-dimensional faces and scenes in pumpkins using tools as simple as kitchen knives or a complex as gouges and chisels. This is a perfect book for woodcarvers who are looking for new and inexpensive ways to celebrate Halloween. While also a great book for Halloween aficionados who are looking for a new way to have the best pumpkin carvings on the block.
ISBN: 1-56523-213-5, 96 pages, Soft Cover, $14.95.

- **Woodcarving the Nativity in the Folk Art Style by Shawn Cipa:** Learn to carve a one-of-a-kind Nativity that will be cherished for years to come. Featuring step-by-step carving and painting instruction for Mary, Joseph, and Baby Jesus and full-sized patterns for the rest of the figures including: Kneeling Angel, Flying Angel, Three Wiseman, Camel, Shepherd and Lamb, Kneeling Shepherd, Sheep, Ox, Donkey and of course, the stable under which they are placed.
ISBN: 1-56523-202-x, 88 pages, soft cover, $14.95.

- **Carving Santas from Around the World by Cyndi Joslyn:** Learn to carve 15 festive Santa's from around the world with this step-by-step guide. Great for beginners, this book begins with an overview of carving tools, materials, safety, transferring patterns, and basic cuts. Then, you'll follow the author as she guides you through 3 projects featuring step-by-step carving and painting instructions. Patterns and photographs for 12 additional projects are included for free-standing and shelf-sitting Santas. Great collectibles!
ISBN: 1-56523-187-2, 112 pages, soft cover, $14.95.

- **Carving Folk Art Figures by Shawn Cipa:** Complete step-by-step carving and painting demonstrations for a folk-art Santa and a smiling Angel from Santa Carver of the Year, Shawn Cipa. Patterns and photographs for an additional 13 projects including Moon Man, Cupid Cat, Firewood Santa, and others also included.
ISBN: 1-56523-171-6, 80 pages, soft cover, $14.95.

- **Bottle Stoppers: Classic Carving Projects Made Easy by Greg Young:** Learn to carve a festive bottle stopper from start-to-finish with the expert instruction provided in this book. Complete carving demonstration for 2 carving demonstrations (Santa and snowman) and 24 additional patterns included.
ISBN: 1-56523-144-9, 80 pages, soft cover, $14.95.

- **Hand Carving Snowmen & Santas in Wood by Mike Shipley:** Features step-by-step instructions with close-up color photography for two holiday carvings and 13 festive ready-to-use patterns. Also included are tips and techniques to rough-out, paint, and antique your projects!
ISBN: 1-56523-129-5, 64 pages, soft cover, $14.95.

CHECK WITH YOUR LOCAL WOODWORKING STORE OR BOOK RETAILER
Or call 800-457-9112 • Visit www.foxchapelpublishing.com